AF700526

To my mother, Marian, for giving me an insatiable desire to learn more and use it to make earth a better place to live; to Eric Kelly, Jerry Knox, and Riad Mahayni for making it possible for me to correct a mistake I made 25 years ago; and to Carol and Pi for giving me the time to do this when time has become so precious.

Regulating Home-Based Businesses in the Twenty-First Century

Charles Wunder, AICP

TABLE OF CONTENTS

Regulating Home-Based Businesses in the Twenty-First Century

Imagine that you are a Zoning Administrator or enforcement officer in Oak Park, Illinois, in the early twentieth century. (Of course, that also means imagining that zoning existed back in those days.) Now imagine that your boss sends you out to 851 Chicago Avenue to investigate an illegal home occupation. After a knock on the door, the owner appears, and you have to talk to him.

"Mr. Wright? Can I call you Frank? OK, Mr. Frank Lloyd Wright, this is the third time I have been out here, and if you don't correct this zoning violation by Friday, I am going to have to write you up. You can have one nonresident employee. We have seen at least five people come everyday, and some days there are more. We know that they are your employees. Your clients are coming here all of the time. You have other architects, engineers, and construction material sales people coming here all the time. Your neighbors are getting fed up with all the traffic.

You have put this huge addition on your house and it is full of drafting tables and equipment. Drafting tables are not equipment found in a typical home. According to the ordinance, they are not allowed. If you want to draw plans, use the kitchen table. We know you are using the extra room for business purposes. According to our building permit records, the room is much larger than the 300 square feet that we allow for home occupation areas. Turn it into a game room, turn it in to a bedroom, turn it into a living room, I don't care! But you can't use it for business purposes. And you'll need to take out this door; you cannot have a separate entrance for your home occupation. Yeah, it will look a little strange, but you should have thought of that before you put it in."

I never met Frank Lloyd Wright, but from what I have read and heard about him, he could be what I will politely call a very "difficult" citizen. There was one way to do things and that was the "Wright" way. No matter. The bottom line is that, if you had been successful in closing down this home occupation, you might have ruined the career of one of the twentieth century's great architects. If you had moved the scene (and the zoning laws) to France, it could have been Claude Monet, the painter, instead. He painted outdoors, another home occupation violation.

These days, you might end up stunting the career of a future Bill Gates (and some people might not think that was all bad) or shutting down a budding Amazon.com. The phenomenal development and increased use of the personal computer have brought new attention to the concept of operating a business out of the home. Computers have given individuals the ability to operate an array of businesses and business activities in the home. The same technological advances and other economic factors (offshore sourcing, for instance) have allowed businesses to pare their workforce, meaning that many individuals have been forced to start their own business at home. In fact, IDC/Link Resources reported in *Entrepreneur* magazine that 30 percent of all who lose their jobs due to downsizing start their own home-based business. And, finally, some corporations have established "satellite" offices for their employees in the employees' residence to save on costs like rent and other ratables (i.e., things that can be measured and taxed). In other words, the way that businesses operate has changed dramatically in the last 10 years, and it appears that this change will continue.

IDC/Link Resources reported in Entrepreneur *magazine that 30 percent of all who lose their jobs due to downsizing start their own home-based business.*

The U.S. Department of Labor study, *Work at Home* in 1997 (available at http://stats.bls.gov/news.release/homey.ws.htm), and the Current Population Survey (available at www.bls.census.gov/cps/cpsmain.htm) illustrate the changing nature of where we work. According to the 1997 survey, 6.1 million U.S. households (approximately 6 percent of all households) contain home-based businesses. A total of 23.3 million people do some work at home. This number may seem large, but it includes full- and part-time workers. Of this 23.3 million, 11.1 million are wage and salary workers who are not expressly paid for the work they do at home (what are now commonly called telecommuters). The 12.2 million workers who do paid work from their homes make up 9 percent of the 135-million-member U.S. workforce.

More than half of the individuals who are self-employed in the U.S. (i.e., about 6.5 million people or 5 percent of the entire workforce) do some work at home. Most home-based businesses (4.1 million) are operated by self-employed individuals. About half of the self-employed individuals who operate a home-based business work full time, and half work part time. The ownership of home-based businesses is fairly evenly split between men and women. Of the self-employed who operate home-based businesses, 1.7 million are managers and professionals, 726,000 are in the construction industry, and 532,000 are in retail sales. The Labor Department study also found that the number of telecommuters grew from 1.9 million in 1991 to 3.6 million in 1997.

Other resources indicate that the U.S. Department of Labor estimates may be low. In 1998, for instance, Wells Fargo Bank conducted a study for the National Federation of Independent Business that indicated that an estimated 3.5 million new businesses were started in that year. Suffice it to say that the number of telecommuters and home-based businesses is extremely large and growing. These numbers would expand significantly if we included the persons, often hobbyists, who occasionally might supplement their income with a sale or two of some craft item.

Publications catering to home-based business operators have joined the frequent media articles on starting and operating a home-based business. Examples include *Home Office Computing* and Svoboda's *Home and Small Business.* Computer magazines, such as *PC Computing, Windows and Windows Sources*, have feature articles and columns for home-based businesses. Business publications like the *Wall Street Journal* and *Business Week* have reported on this phenomenon. Suddenly, because "dream" technology has become affordable for individuals and small businesses, more and more people are choosing to operate their own companies, marking a new age of entrepreneurialism, new products, and new services.

Many local Chambers of Commerce have programs and services geared for home-based businesses. Several organizations have formed in recent years to represent the interests of home-based businesses. They include the American Association of Home-Based Businesses www.aahbb.org/), the Home-Based Business Council (www.medusaonline.com/hbbc), and the Small Office Home Office Knowledge Center (www.so-ho.org/).

Some of the "how-to" articles include warnings and sometimes disparaging remarks about local land-use controls that affect home-based businesses and home offices. Stories about home-based businesses often include anecdotes of conflicts with local planning departments. In a *Home Office Computing* article (February 1993), "Home Business Outlaws" by Mary McAleer Vizard (1993), Chicago realtor Terri Murphy, commenting on the unrealistically low limits on the number of customers or people working in a home contained in some ordinances, says, "Those kinds of rules make no sense to me. My mother has more people than that coming over for coffee." Home-based business operators are not the only source of criticism. In the same article, Louis Goodman, Director of Building in New Rochelle, New York, states, "With archaic businesses, such as milliners on the books, obviously, the code needs to better reflect the times." In a *Nation's Business* article (February 1995), "Beyond the Nuts and Bolts," Ripley Hotch writes, "Still in many jurisdictions, local officials take a dim view of commercial activity in a neighborhood. You should check with the zoning authorities at city hall or your county government to make sure that you aren't breaking any laws." The perception seems to be—and some of the examples indicate that it may be true—that most zoning ordinances inhibit home-based businesses.

Chicago realtor Terri Murphy, commenting on the unrealistically low limits on the number of customers or people working in a home contained in some ordinances, says, "Those kinds of rules make no sense to me. My mother has more people than that coming over for coffee."

As a zoning administrator in Bolingbrook, Illinois (a Chicago suburb), and McLean County, Illinois (a rural county), I found that citizen inquiries about working in the home were becoming more common and frequent. It also became obvious that there were more businesses that didn't fit into old classifications. The old home occupation regulations often had conflicting provisions with unintended consequences. What had served as a reasonable (and relatively successful) accommodation of business activity in the home in the past was now badly out of date due to changes in the way modern businesses operate.

Over the past 30 years, I have operated a number of home-based businesses, including a planning consulting business and an art studio. Both are examples of business activities allowed by many zoning ordinance home occupation regulations. However, I have found a number of routine practices in both professions that technically violate home occupation regulations typical in many communities. Although my violations weren't apparent to anybody but me and there were no impacts on my neighbors, I knew that I was in violation and I was not entirely comfortable with that knowledge. I took little comfort in knowing that if Frank Lloyd Wright and Claude Monet were alive and working in the United States today, they would probably be violating the local zoning regulations.

Certainly, as a planner as well as a home business operator, what I have discovered is that many communities need to do a better job of consulting with home business operators to get their input.

This report is intended as a guide for zoning and planning officials who want to update their zoning regulations for home-based businesses. It is based on a study of zoning regulations in DuPage County, Illinois, and a study of effective home-based business regulations from a number of U.S. municipalities and counties provided by the Planning Advisory Service staff. The results of my study of both sets of regulations and my own business experiences led me to develop some principles that helped me form a set of guidelines that planners can use as a basis to develop regulations appropriate to their community's circumstances. Certainly, as a planner as well as a home business operator, what I have discovered is that many communities need to do a better job of consulting with home business operators to get their input on what regulations would be effective and what incentives government can offer to home businesses that opt to become registered and licensed. Without that input, tailoring effective regulations for home occupations becomes more of a trial-and-error process than it may need to be.

The first section of this report, Literature Review, focuses on four areas: the origination of home occupation regulations, a review of the subject of home occupation regulations in some of the major land-use law treatises, and a review of past PAS reports on home occupations and other publications. The second section focuses on a study of 27 home occupation ordinances from a wide variety of jurisdictions. This section will also include a critique of these ordinances and a brief discussion of a similar study of home occupation regulations in DuPage County, Illinois. The final section presents a regulatory framework for governing home-based business activities, provides a range of available options for use within that framework, and closes with a "manual" for adapting this framework and these suggestions to your local situation.

LITERATURE REVIEW

Bassett (1940) described development of home occupation provisions in the first comprehensive zoning ordinances. References to his discussion of home occupation provisions appears in a number of early court decisions and legal treatises on zoning and land-use controls.

Bassett said that the development of such regulations was a mechanism to allow a variety of nonconforming uses in residential zoning districts that differentiated between nonconforming uses that the jurisdiction wanted to eliminate and nonconforming uses that it not only did not intend to eliminate but, in fact, it wanted to encourage.

> The earliest zoning ordinances took communities as they existed and did not try to prevent customary practices that met with no objection from the community. Indeed, there would have been great opposition to early zoning plans if efforts had been made to prevent doctors or dressmakers from using their own homes in residential districts.

The nonconforming uses to be eliminated were ones that had disruptive effects on the surrounding residences. Examples would include grocery stores that generated enough car or truck traffic to become nuisances in a residential setting or small factories. These were labeled nonconforming uses and made subject to provisions that would lead to their elimination. The nonconforming uses to be allowed included the offices of "professionals," artists, teachers, and dressmakers. They were characterized by three conditions:

1. That the use must be customary in a residence (that is, customary for that time period, the 1920s)

2. That the use be incidental to the primary residential use
3. That the home occupation not be a business

It is important to recognize the nuances in Bassett's use of the words "business" and "professional" and their role in the early home occupation regulations. It seems to be the origin of some of the inconsistencies in today's home occupation regulations. If a person painted a landscape or portrait, they were considered an artist, one of the very limited number of professions and, thus, the operator of a permitted home occupation. If the image that person painted said "For Sale", they were considered a sign painter, a business, and, thus, a prohibited home occupation.

A fairly large percentage of the court decisions involving "home occupations" have dealt with the question of whether a particular use was a "profession " and/or a "business." For the most part, the courts and popular culture have expanded the common definition of "professional" over the years.

There were few basic changes in home occupation regulations in the first few decades of zoning. Some of this may be attributable to the disruptions of the economic depression of the 1930s and World War II. The "business models" of that time were fairly static and relatively limited by available technology and communication and transportation systems. After World War II, a number of changes in those factors led to a new spatial independence for the business world, which in turn led to new business "models."

Incremental changes in home occupation regulations began appearing in the 1960s. As early as 1966, Davenport, Iowa, amended its zoning ordinance to differentiate between home occupations and home offices. The 1970s and 1980s saw home day care introduced into many home occupation regulations. As the personal computer became more common as a business tool, another wave of home occupation amendments developed in the 1980s.

It is important to recognize the nuances in Bassett's use of the words "business" and "professional" and their role in the early home occupation regulations. It seems to be the origin of some of the inconsistencies in today's home occupation regulations.

Legal Treatises

Over the years, there have been numerous court decisions dealing with business activities in the home. Most of the major legal treatises on zoning include discussions of home occupation regulations. Often, they are included within a more inclusive subject area, accessory uses.

Patrick Rohan's *Zoning and Land-Use Controls* (1977, with annual supplements) contains a relatively brief discussion of home occupation regulations. He starts with the "customary" mention that the home occupation be customarily incidental to the residence and that the operator be an occupant of that residence. He cites nine cases from a number of states that deal with and support this concept.[1] A discussion of limitations on permitted employees follows. He cites cases from Arkansas, Colorado, and Tennessee addressing this concept.[2] The next limitation that Rohan discusses relates to the appearance of the residence containing the home occupation. The language in the ordinances being reviewed by the courts dealt with signage, separate entrances, and the display of goods for sale. He lists two legal citations from Louisiana addressing these limitations.[3] Finally, Rohan reviews the issue of limiting the equipment used in the home occupation and permitted "professions." He includes 20 cases covering a wide variety of prohibited and permitted home occupations, including physicians, attorneys, veterinarians, music teachers, dance teachers, artists, real estate brokers, insurance agents, and printers.

Arden and Daren Rathkopf in the *Law of Zoning and Planning* (1975 with annual supplements) discuss home occupations in the section on accessory uses. Early in that section, they state:

> The use of a building as a residence necessarily involves, to a greater or lesser extent, some business activity. An attorney may discuss legal matters with a friend or client, a salesman may compute his commissions or plan his forthcoming calls within the confines of his home, an architect may draw plans or a businessman may go over his accounts. These quasi-business uses are permissible as long as the type and magnitude of the business uses are such as to render them incidental to the primary residential use.

They cite several cases that address the secondary, incidental nature of the home occupation and specifically cite two cases in which the courts ruled that the activity in question was incidental and secondary to the primary residential use.[4] They provide a far greater number of citations for cases in which the courts have ruled that the business activities have exceeded allowable limits.[5]

The second issue that the Rathkops discuss is that the home occupation be conducted by the person living in the residence. The cases that establish the requirement that the home occupation operator reside on premise include one in which a dentist's office was judged to be a suitable home occupation.[6]

The final area that they focus on is the concept of "professional uses." They cite three cases where courts addressed the validity of permitting exceptions to the purely residential uses allowed in residential zoning districts.[7] They then review two sub-areas of this subject. The first concerns the level of activity or magnitude of a permitted "profession" becoming something that is prohibited.[8] The second concern with the issue of what "professional" does and doesn't include.[9]

Robert M. Anderson's *American Law of Zoning* (1986) includes the language from a number of specific ordinances to illustrate his discussion of home occupation regulations. After the now familiar quote from Bassett, Anderson cites various ordinances that limit home occupations to customary, incidental activities accessory to the residential use. He also includes language from a Michigan decision that addresses this concept.[10]

Anderson goes on to include an analysis of a profession as a home occupation and what has been and has not been considered a "profession." The case law is too extensive to be included in this review. If the reader is interested in examining several cases addressing the issue of individual professions and home occupations, Anderson's publication is a good place to start.

The subject of doctors, dentists, and surgeons is covered in Section 10.04 where several ordinances that specifically list them as permitted home occupations are cited. His discussion also covers several cases dealing with the concept of permitting a doctor's office while prohibiting a medical clinic. It also deals with related areas, such as area and employee limitations. Sections 10.05, 10.06, 10.07, and 10.08 address the subject of veterinarians, attorneys, engineers/architects, and accountants as professions and, thus, a permitted home occupation.

In Sections 10.09, Anderson cites ordinances that treat real estate offices as home occupations. He also cites four cases dealing with the question of real estate as a profession when it has not specifically been listed in the ordinance. Section 10.010 deals with insurance agencies in a similar manner.

In Sections 10.011, 10.12, and 10.13, the subject of music, dance and artists studios, respectively, are covered. Studios traditionally have been considered a customary home occupation and Anderson cites several zoning ordinances specifically permitting them. He also cites several court cases that have placed some limitations on studios as places of instruction.

The third component of Anderson's analysis covers other uses that have been traditionally addressed in home occupation regulations. These include barbershops, beauty parlors, dressmakers, baby-sitting, funeral homes, boarding and rooming houses, and nursing and convalescent homes among others. As in the previous sections, Anderson quotes a number of ordinances containing language governing the listed uses.

Section 10.14 includes an extensive discussion of the subject of barbershops and beauty shops. He starts by stating that barber and beauty shops were common home-based businesses before zoning began. He cites zoning ordinances that specifically permit and some that specifically prohibit them as home occupations. The bulk of the litigation dealing with this matter generally involves zoning ordinances that do not specifically address this use. He cites a number of cases that have not recognized a beauty shop as a customary home occupation and some that have.

Dressmaking and babysitting are discussed in Sections 10.15 and 10.16, respectively. Although undoubtedly a trade or business, dressmaking and tailoring have traditionally been home occupations. Although Anderson cites a couple of zoning ordinances that have listed it as a permitted home occupation, he does not cite any court cases involving this use. Probably a reflection of the date it was written (1968), Anderson dismisses babysitting as an informal arrangement and doesn't even mention day care. He does cite one case in which a "nursery" was recognized as a permitted home occupation.

Section 10.17 discusses the subject of funeral homes. Anderson states that the courts have consistently found that funeral homes were a trade or business rather than a permitted "profession." Parking and traffic problems and the disposal of waste materials from the undertaking process make this an obvious candidate for exclusion.

Section 10.18 deals with boarding/rooming houses. Anderson recognizes that zoning ordinances have dealt with boarding/rooming houses in a number of different ways. He notes that they may be prohibited as a home occupation but listed as a permitted use in some of the less restrictive residential zoning districts. Much of Anderson's discussion on boarding/rooming houses centers on the area of what they are and are not. Nursing and convalescent homes are dealt with in Section 10.19. Again, a reflection of its age, the book makes no mention of group homes in this section.

The last component of Anderson's chapter on home occupations addresses other limitations common to many home occupation regulations. They include location, area, number of employees, mechanical equipment, stock-in-trade, and limitations on alterations to the exterior of the house. In each he gives examples of the specific ordinance language used to limit activities along with the courts decision.

At first glance it might appear that court decisions involving home occupation regulations have been anything but consistent. The courts' decisions have allowed and prohibited beauty shops and barbershops as home occupations. They have allowed and prohibited home occupations to be conducted in an accessory structure. Some decisions have been more liberal in interpreting the term "professional" than others.

But it is not the decisions that have been inconsistent—it has been the ordinances that regulate home occupations. The court decisions begin to

As is often the case with terms that cannot be quantitatively defined, the term "customary" is open to interpretation; in this case, the definition of "customary" is related to an era or specific time and its cultural and economic characteristics.

have a more consistent pattern when you examine the decision and what that particular ordinance allowed or didn't allow. If the home occupation regulations specifically allowed a beauty/barber shop, the courts have generally upheld their inclusion as home occupations. In most cases, the courts have been remarkably consistent in upholding whatever is contained in the local home occupation regulations.

If the regulations don't specifically address an issue, the courts have tended to base their decisions on the core principle that home occupations are customary, incidental, and secondary to the primary residential use. There seems to be some importance given to the specific characteristics of specific home occupation (i.e., whether it was a one-chair beauty shop with very few customers or a three-chair shop with employees and a lot of customers). As is often the case with terms that cannot be quantitatively defined, the term "customary" is open to interpretation; in this case, the definition of "customary" is related to an era or specific time and its cultural and economic characteristics. What was once "customary" may now be completely outmoded, and what is "new" (using that term as the opposite of customary) might be a more appropriate occupation for a home business. This is why regulations need regular review and why exclusionary lists of very specific permitted uses are not a good idea—a subject that is covered in greater detail below.

APA Publications

APA has published three Planning Advisory Service monographs as well as other works on home occupation regulations since the 1950s.

Zoning Regulations of Home Occupations (PAS Report No. 54, September 1953) discusses the basis for home occupations: that the use is customary, incidental (or accessory), and is not a business. This publication was the first to question the distinction between a business and a profession.

> However, it is not clear that overt physical characteristics are always significant reasons for discriminating between the "professions" and the "customary home occupations." And it is not certain that some businesses are more objectionable in these terms than some professions.

The publication looks at various zoning regulations in 11 areas of home occupation activities. The concluding discussion of the future course of home occupation regulations stated:

> We seem, therefore, to have reached a fork in the road. One way leads down the classical path of custom and incidentalness. The other departs from custom, retains incidentalness, and takes on specification (and perhaps even performance) criteria. For each community, a decision on the path to be followed rests on its answer to a constant, fundamental question: What is the proper use of land in a residential district? Shall it be wholly and exclusively residential, or shall nonresidential uses compatible with dwellings be permitted? If nonresidential uses are permitted, what basis for their authorization shall be used? Shall any use (including manufacturing perhaps) be permitted so long as it is in harmony with the comprehensive plan? or Shall nonresidential uses be limited to those that are functionally related to dwellings and which need the same kind of environment, such as churches, schools, and hospitals?

Planning for Home Occupations by William Toner (PAS Report No. 316, April 1976) starts with a rather sharp attack on the Chicago home occupation regulations, specifically, and all home occupation regulations in general.

> First, the most important problem and the one which plagues most ordinances is simply that the ordinance bears only the slightest relationship to the public interest. Many ordinances, including Chicago's, would technically prohibit a person like Saul Bellow from writing full time in his home. Clearly, any city would have a hard time defending such an ordinance in court, much less in the court of common sense.

Toner goes on to write, "The home occupation provision is perhaps the most consistently violated section of the zoning ordinance." He identifies three other primary problems:

1. The average person does not know what a home occupation is or that home occupation regulations exist.
2. The average person does not know who to ask about home occupation regulations or avoids asking the questions because he is afraid that the answer will be no.
3. The ordinances are full of clumsy, vague language.

The home occupation provision is perhaps the most consistently violated section of the zoning ordinance.

Toner offers two approaches to the regulation of home occupations: a permit approach and a no-permit approach. He believes that in communities where permits are required, the ordinances tend to rely on performance standards. In communities where no permit is required, the ordinances rely heavily on lists of permitted and prohibited uses. The next two chapters and the appendix in Toner's report provide excerpts from several ordinances.

PAS Report No. 391 (October 1985), *Home Occupation Ordinances*, by JoAnn Butler and Judith Getzels was the first PAS Report to discuss the coming changes brought by technological advances. After a brief introduction, the authors offered this criticism of home occupation ordinances:

> One of the difficulties with current ordinances is that they do not always reflect today's workplace. Many of the changes in the nature of home-based work have occurred so rapidly that local zoning regulations have not caught up with them. People who try to work at home complain that they are either prevented from pursuing occupations for reasons that are not clear to them or that large numbers of home occupations take place illegally—putting those that stay within the law at an unfair disadvantage.

Their criticism is similar to that of Toner's 10 years earlier. If the criticisms are taken as valid, it would appear that little progress was made in modernizing home occupation ordinances. The 1985 publication also gives a brief summary of a 1984 survey of the home occupation ordinances in the 1,100 communities that subscribed to PAS.

> In scrutinizing the nearly 600 home occupation ordinances received from the survey respondents, APA found that the ordinances typically contained these elements:
>
> 1. a definition of home occupations;
> 2. the background or history preceding the ordinance enactment or amendment;
> 3. an intent and purpose or policy statement describing why home occupations were being regulated in the community;
> 4. a listing of permitted and prohibited home occupations;
> 5. a series of conditions or set of performance standards that home occupations must meet;

6. a statement of review procedures applied to home occupation; and
7. enforcement procedures.

Very few home occupation ordinances received by APA contained all these elements. However, those ordinances that provided the clearest guidance to both zoning regulators and potential home-based business persons contained most of these elements.

The format of home occupation ordinances has changed little since 1953. One of the most striking discoveries of the literature review process was that current criticisms of home occupation ordinances are nearly identical to those made in 1976 and 1985.

The elements listed above indicate that the format of home occupation ordinances has changed little since 1953. One of the most striking discoveries of the literature review process was that current criticisms of home occupation ordinances are nearly identical to those made in 1976 and 1985. Despite the fact that the authors of these works pointed to the changes that needed to be made to compose fairer, more comprehensive, more modern home occupation regulations, the planning community has not seen fit to make those changes. This has resulted in an unpleasant situation for both the administrators of the zoning ordinance and the home-based business operator. Many existing home-based businesses are operating illegally without having any adverse impacts on the surrounding neighborhood. Zoning administrators are routinely forced to ignore the zoning ordinance or impose unreasonable regulations on modern business practices.

The technological changes noted in the Butler and Getzels PAS Report led to more consideration of home occupations in other APA publications in the 1980s and afterwards. The January 1984 issue of the *PAS Memo* by Frederick Allen III dealt with performance standards for home occupations. It references the changing nature of the American economy evolving from a manufacturing base to a service economy. It also refers to advances in computer technology as potential change agents in the way we do business and where we do business. Allen noted the limitations imposed on "new professions" by the use of the word "customary" in home occupation regulations. He wrote, "The point is that ordinances that permit 'customary' uses do little except set the scene for a law suit to determine whether a particular use is customary or not." The article also contains a very simple "model" of home occupation regulations. The article was accompanied by a bibliography by Gregory Longhini that references the legal treatises by Patrick Rohan, Robert Anderson, and Norman Williams.

The March 1984 issue of *Zoning News* contains an interesting glimpse into the development and evolution of home occupation regulations in the mid-1980s. Reporting on the state of these regulations, the article notes three trends. The first was that the home occupation regulations were getting more detailed. The second was that some home occupation regulations were differentiating between different levels of intensity or magnitude. Ordinances began to allow some uses by right, while others created a registration process or a public approval process involving a hearing before a board. Having different home occupation regulations for different kinds of agricultural and residential zoning districts also became more common.

Zoning News (December 1991), "When Home Is Where the Business Is," discusses state-of-the-art home occupation regulations. It discusses definitions and permits, lists of permitted and prohibited uses versus standards, home occupation regulations for rural areas, and enforcement issues.

Most recently, Mark Dennison addressed "Home Occupations as Accessory Uses" in the January 1996 issue of *Zoning News*. It covers many of the areas mentioned in the previous articles. Most notable is a sidebar at the end of the article including several late 1980s and 1990s court decisions relating to home occupations.

The 1990s saw two articles in the Planning Practice feature in *Planning* magazine. The first, "Homework," by Michael Frank appeared in the June 1993. Frank developed a model for regulating eight "categories" of permitted home occupations. They included professional offices, personal services, instructional services, home craft businesses, family day care, trades businesses, and repair services. Each of these sections includes a thorough discussion of what may or may not be permitted and possible conditions for approval for these businesses.

The May 1999 Planning Practice feature, "Home Bodies" by Julie Bennett, is an extensive and current look at the subject of home-based business activities and current home occupation regulations. After introductory comments from two very different perspectives, the article follows with a discussion of two New Jersey statutes governing home-based businesses statewide. The article then reviews the efforts of a couple of communities that created some innovative regulations to deal with both new and existing home-based businesses. The article also discussed some of the administrative and enforcement implications of different types of ordinances.

It may be time to look at home occupation regulations in the context of planning's latest trend, neotraditional planning or New Urbanism.

The April 1997 issue of APA's Economic Development Division newsletter contains three articles on home-based work issues. "Home-Based Business and Welfare Reform: The Case of the GVM Market in Richmond, Virginia" by John Arccordino examines the potential for home-based businesses to provide jobs and job training in areas of chronically high levels of unemployment. A program in Richmond, Virginia, is examined as another option in providing needed business services and goods in some public housing areas. "Home-Based Work and the Community" by Kathryn Stafford, Alma Owen, and Suzanne Loker reports on data gathered on the impacts of home-based work on communities. The data includes information on the extent and characteristics of home-based work. "Home-Based Work and Zoning" by an unidentified author focuses its study on two "distressed" communities in Baltimore. The author cites four common problems with home-based businesses, including parking, hours of operation, noise, and signage. The author proposes a two-tiered regulatory system to minimize negative impacts on the surrounding neighborhoods.

Susan Handy and Patricia Mokhtatian outline some problems and concerns dealing with telecommuting in "Planning for Telecommuting—Measurement and Policy Issues," in the *Journal of the American Planning Association* in Winter 1995. They included then-current data on home-based work. They discuss the problems of measuring telecommuting due to the wide variations in how much time is spent in the home office or remote location versus in the business's offices. The article closes with a very interesting discussion of the various policy issues involved with telecommuting. While recognizing the more commonly known environmental and social benefits associated with telecommuting, the authors also make note of a possible negative consequence. They express some concern that telecommuting facilitates and thus encourages low-density sprawl by eliminating one of sprawl's negative consequences, a long and aggravating commute.

With that in mind, it may be time to look at home occupation regulations in the context of planning's latest trend, neotraditional planning or New Urbanism. One of the hallmarks of this concept has been its criticism of the segregation of differing land uses in the "suburban" model. In investigating this area, it is important to make careful distinctions regulating the mixing of land uses. Home occupations, by definition, are often accessory uses in a residential zoning district. Residences as an accessory or secondary use in a commercial zoning district are an entirely, and distinctly, different regulatory challenge.

A STUDY AND ANALYSIS OF HOME OCCUPATION REGULATIONS

DuPage County

My interest in home occupation regulations became more extensive in the mid-1990s when I chose this area as my thesis topic at Iowa State University. I decided to study 27 municipal zoning ordinances in suburban DuPage County, Illinois. I examined all 27 home occupation regulations in terms of 11 regulatory categories. The study included criticisms and, in a few cases, praise of the language used in the ordinances. It also included a "model" ordinance for dealing with home-based businesses.

My thesis contained an "accessory" study in an appendix. The inclusion of that study had more to do with a personal curiosity about the impacts of home occupations than the primary academic work at hand. The study used the DuPage County Geographic Information System to study the impacts of home occupations on communities. A business database provided by the State of Illinois and incorporated into the Geographic Information System provided me with site-specific information on the type of business being conducted, the number of employees, and the annual sales of the businesses. In addition to the business information on properties zoned for residential uses, the Geographic Information System allowed me to look for correlations between the number of home-based businesses, residential property values, and vacancy rates.

Each ordinance was given a numerical rating on a permissive/restrictive continuum based on a four-level score in each of the 11 regulatory categories (see the section below for a description of these categories). The data was then examined for correlations between the permissiveness or restrictiveness of ordinances and the number of home-based businesses, the number of home-based business employees, home-based business sales, residential property values, and housing vacancy rates.

The data may indicate, and I can't stress the "may" enough, that there are some weak positive correlations between the ordinances and their economic impacts. The data may also indicate there is a weak positive correlation between the number of home-based businesses and residential property values. This may have been expected because of the large percentage of the home-based business types in the professional/managerial category. My "accessory" study should be examined with a healthy level of skepticism. The study was undertaken in my rather limited spare time, with out-of-pocket funding, using preexisting data and questionable data completeness and/or quality. The database originated with Dunn and Bradstreet and was based on business credit information. Without question, this didn't present a truly representative sample of home-based businesses in DuPage County. In all likelihood, it did not contain a lot of new, independently financed or part-time home-based businesses. Yet, my gut feeling is that a more rigorous study would come to similar conclusions.

I was expecting significant economic impacts related to home-based businesses, but I was completely surprised by some of the results (and their implications). I had more than 3,000 businesses in my database, and the average number of employees per home-based business was greater than five. It wasn't particularly uncommon to see businesses with more than 100 employees. This seemed more than a little unusual considering that most of the home occupation regulations limited the number of nonresident employees to one. It certainly appeared that large numbers of zoning violators were "invisible" to the local zoning authorities.

The amounts of the annual sales of these home-based businesses were equally staggering. The total annual sales in individual communities ranged up to $600 million in Hinsdale. Granted, these are sales figures and not profits. Planners who tend to think of home-based businesses as providing minimal economic benefits/impacts on the local business community may need to rethink this assumption.

A National Review

I used a similar approach to the one I used in the DuPage County study to examine the home occupation regulations from 27 zoning ordinances provided by the Planning Advisory Service staff. Six county zoning ordinances were included. The 27 ordinances represent a variety of types of jurisdictions, using geography and population size as criteria. (See Table 1.)

I used 11 subject categories to examine the ordinances in an organized manner.

1. *Stratification*. Measures the extent to which the ordinance contains provisions that differentiate levels or magnitudes of business activities within and across zoning districts. Such ordinances would include language that would provide for things like home occupations by right or through staff, zoning board, or legislative approval and the application of different standards or conditions to similar uses in different zoning districts.

2. *Location/area.* Refers to the presence of provisions that: require residence of the employees in the house where the home-based business is taking place; address whether the home occupation can be conducted in an accessory structure; and specify limits on the percentage of structure area or area taken up by the home occupation.

3. *Employees*. Indicates if the ordinance limits the numbers of resident and nonresident employees.

4. *Customer/hours.* Refers to the presence of provisions that prohibit or limit the number of clients/customers at any one time and/or on a daily basis, and the hours that the business may have customers or clients visit.

5. *Signage/exterior alterations.* Indicates whether the ordinance prohibits or limits the area of signage, separate entrances for the home occupation, and the display of goods for sale.

6. *Sales.* A category that covers a wide range of ordinance language, including provisions distinguishing between retail, wholesale, phone, and on-premise sales. Some ordinances included some of their sales limitations within a prohibited or permitted use list. This category would also consider provisions limiting sales to goods produced on the premises.

7. *Parking/delivery vehicles.* Covers provisions that regulate on and off-street customer parking, parking setbacks, and number and size of delivery and business vehicles.

8. *Nuisances/equipment*. This category is closely related to the parking/delivery vehicle category. It indicates whether the ordinance has provisions imposing limits on the types of equipment and machinery that can be used in a home occupation, and the noise, vibrations, odors, smoke, and electrical interference that the home occupation may generate.

9. *Permitted use list.* Self-explanatory.

10. *Prohibited use list.* Self-explanatory.

11. *Administration.* Covers the various provisions that require some form of registration or recorded approval, including references to other governmental requirements, such as business licenses, health department regulations, and fire and life/safety codes.

Table 1 shows the results of my analysis of the 27 communities ordinances along with the jurisdiction names.

TABLE 1. CATEGORICAL PROVISIONS WITHIN HOME OCCUPATION ORDINANCE

	Stratification	Location/area	Employees	Customer/hours limits	Signage/exterior alterations	Sales	Parking/delivery vehicles	Nuisances/equipment	Permitted use list	Prohibited use list	Administration
Blue Springs, Missouri		X	X		X	X	X	X		X	X
Chicago, Ill.		X	X	X	X	X	X	X	X	X	X
Carona, Calif.		X	X	X	X	X	X	X	X		
Cumra Township, Pa.		X		X		X					
Dade County, Fla.		X	X		X	X	X	X	X	X	X
Danville, Ill.	X	X	X	X	X	X	X	X	X	X	X
DuPage County, Ill.		X	X	X	X	X	X	X		X	
Eau Claire, Wisc.		X	X	X	X	X	X	X		X	X
Edmunds, Wash.		X	X	X	X	X		X			X
Hinsdale, Ill.		X	X	X	X	X	X	X			
Jacksonville, N.C.		X	X		X	X	X	X		X	X
Jefferson County, Colo.	X	X			X		X	X	X	X	
Junction City, Ore.		X	X	X	X			X			
Marion, Iowa		X	X		X			X		X	
Morgantown, W. Va.		X	X		X	X	X	X			X
Naperville, Ill.		X	X	X	X	X		X	X	X	
Niskayuma, N.Y.		X	X		X		X	X	X	X	
Ogden City, Utah		X	X		X	X					X
Rochingham County, Va.	X	X	X	X	X			X			
Roswell, N.M.		X	X	X	X	X	X	X	X	X	X
Santa Clara, Calif.		X	X		X	X	X	X			X
Satelitte Beach, Fla.		X	X	X	X	X	X	X		X	X
Scott County, Ill.		X	X		X			X			
Stanislaus County, Calif.		X	X	X	X			X		X	
Tacoma, Wash.		X	X		X	X		X			X
Wolfeboro, N.H.		X	X		X	X					
Woodridge, Ill.		X	X	X	X				X	X	

As the table shows, the vast majority of the surveyed ordinances contained provisions dealing with location/area limitations, employees, signage and exterior alterations, and nuisance and equipment prohibitions. Fewer ordinances include provisions dealing with customer/hours limitations, sales limitations, parking and delivery vehicle regulations, prohibited uses, and administration. Only nine ordinances contained lists of permitted uses, and only three ordinances used stratification to deal with home-based businesses.

Working from this general list, I break down each category in the following sections of the report, indicating the range of regulatory options, from restrictive to permissive and from specific to general, used by these communities.

Stratification

Only three of the 27 communities stratified their home-based business regulations. The Danville, Illinois, zoning ordinance was the only ordinance that set up "minor" and "major" home occupations, each with its own standards and requirements. Jefferson County, Colorado, and Rockingham County, Virginia, had a provision that allowed a Zoning Board of Adjustment/County Board to approve "home occupations" that did not meet the performance standards or were not on the "permitted use" list contained in the ordinance.

Location/Area

Provisions related to location and area limits were found in 26 of the 27 ordinances. There were some variations in the way the communities addressed this condition. Table 2 provides a more specific breakdown.

All of the 27 home occupation regulations had provisions that required the business activities be conducted within the primary or accessory structures. Fourteen (51 percent) of the ordinances limited the home occupation to the primary residential structure, while 11 (41 percent) allowed accessory structures to be used. Twenty-three (85 percent) of the ordinances imposed additional area limitations in the form of specific area or percentage limits. Only three of the ordinances included both specific area limits and a cap on the percentage of area that could be used to house a home-based business. With one exception, the ordinances didn't contain any surprises and probably reflect a good cross section of what is being used today. The Woodridge, Illinois, ordinance did specify that the exterior of the residence could be used under certain conditions.

TABLE 2. LOCATION AND AREA LIMITS

Type of limit	Number of ordinances containing this limit
Primary structure	16
Primary and accessory structure	11
Area percentage limit	16
Specific area limit	4
Area percentage and specific area limits	3

Employees

Table 3 shows the breakdown of regulatory variations dealing with employees. Only the Jefferson County, Colorado, ordinance did not contain any provisions addressing this area. The variations in employee regulations are relatively limited.

The vast majority of the ordinances fall into two groups. Seventeen (63 percent) prohibit all nonresident employees. Only seven (26 percent) limited it to one or two nonresident employees. Most of this second group imposed a limit of one nonresident employee. There were a couple of unusual regulatory variations in this area. Junction City, Utah, specified that two part-time nonresident employees could be substituted for one full-time nonresident employee. Two of the ordinances that banned nonresident employee(s) made an exception for day care facilities. Notably, Hinsdale and Woodridge, Illinois, had language that indicated that the employees who did not work at the location of the home occupation were exempt from these limits.

TABLE 3. EMPLOYEES

Types of limits	Number of ordinances containing this limit
Limited to residents	14
Limited to resident with exceptions	3
One nonresident employee	5
Two nonresident employees	2
Limits only employees working in the home	2

TABLE 4. CUSTOMER VISIT LIMITS

Types of limits	Number of ordinances containing a limit
No or vague provisions	20
Total prohibition of business visitors	1
Hours limitations	1
Total daily limit	3
Limit on total at any one time	3

Customer Visit Limits

Table 4 offers some surprising findings. If these 27 are representative of the home occupation regulation universe, the use of specific customer visitation regulations is relatively uncommon.

Twenty (74 percent) of the ordinances contained no or very vague provisions governing customer or client visits to the home occupation. The "vague" provisions are usually language referring to limitations on traffic generation or pedestrian visits, including the word "typical." Of the ordinances that provide very specific, measurable limits, two groups were apparent: those that regulated a total daily limit, and those that regulated the number of customers present at any one time. There were equal numbers in each of these groups. Only DuPage County also set hours for customer or client visits.

TABLE 5. REGULATIONS ON SALES

Types of limits	Number of ordinances containing a limit
No provisions	10
Limited to goods made on a premise	6
Total prohibition	7
Implied that very limited sales were permitted	4

Regulations on Sales

Table 5 examines home occupation provisions that relate to "sales." These provisions include the total prohibition of sales on the premises to varying levels of permitted sales.

Ten (37 percent) of the ordinances did not have any separate provisions addressing sales. Seven (26 percent) prohibited retail sales entirely. Six (22 percent) permitted the sale of goods made on the premises. The four remaining ordinances fall into what I would call a "an occasional sale is OK" group. They often implied that while sales were not entirely prohibited, they should be considered relatively infrequent events.

TABLE 6. PARKING/DELIVERY PROVISIONS

Types of limit	Number of ordinances containing this limit
No provisions	11
Customer/client parking	10
Limitations on delivery vehicles/times	4
Limitations on commercial vehicles used	4

Parking/Delivery Vehicle Provisions

Table 6 examines the use of regulations related to vehicle use associated with the home occupation. These regulations are composed of three types of restrictions.

These home occupation regulations include provisions in three areas: the parking of customers/clients coming to visit the home occupation, vehicles that are used by the home occupation, and vehicles delivering goods to the home occupation. It seems a little unusual that such a large percentage of the ordinances didn't have any regulations governing vehicular use associated with the home occupations. Eleven (41 percent) had no provisions.

Ten (37 percent) of the ordinances contained some provisions related to customer/client visitation parking. These provisions included the required number of off-street parking spaces and the location of these parking spaces. The moderate number of ordinances with customer parking requirements may be explained by the fact that, if an ordinance is very restrictive in terms of the types of home-based businesses allowed, concern about parking spaces may not be warranted. Four (15 percent) of the ordinances had restrictions on the size and frequency of deliveries, as well as permitted delivery times. Four ordinances also limited the number and/or size of the commercial vehicles used by a home-based business.

TABLE 7. PERMITTED USE LIST

Types of limitations	Number of ordinances containing this limitation
No permitted use list	17
Generalized list	7
Specific list	3

Permitted Uses

I was more than a little surprised by the number of home occupation regulations that did not contain some form of a permitted home occupation list. (See Table 7.) Seventeen (63 percent) of them did not have one. Of the 10 ordinances that had them, seven had lists that were of a more general nature. It may be noteworthy that only three of the ordinances had what I judged to be very specific, exclusive permitted use lists. If this is a representative sample of current home occupation regulations, there may be a movement away from a very specific and limiting permitted use list. It should be noted that several of the home occupation regulations sometimes allowed some specific use (e.g., day care, garage sales, and bed and breakfast establishments in a historic district) in provisions separate from the permitted use list in the home occupation regulations.

Prohibited Uses

Table 8 examines the use of generalized and specific prohibited use lists.

A surprisingly large number of the ordinances, 12 (44 percent) did not contain a separate prohibited list. As expected, most of the home occupation regulations (15 ordinances) did contain some form of a prohibited home occupation list. While these lists most often contained specific uses, they would occasionally make use of more generalized terms, such as the prohibition of retail sales, direct retail sales, repair shops, and the like. There are a number of these uses that vie for the most frequently prohibited home occupation. Auto repair, kennels, stables, beauty salons/barber shops, medical/dental/veterinarian clinics, and funeral homes are among the most widely prohibited uses.

TABLE 8. PROHIBITED USE LIST

Types of limitations	Number of ordinances containing this limitation
No prohibited use list	12
Prohibited use list	15
Barber/beauty shops	8
Auto repair	9

Administration

Table 9 presents the results of my analysis of the 27 ordinances as regards their use of approval and registration mechanisms. Administrative provisions include requirements for licensing or registration. They include referencing licenses from other governmental departments. Among the ordinances that require registration/licensing, there are provisions for staff approvals as well as advisory board/legislative body approvals. A few ordinances distinguished between staff approvals for some home occupation regulations and advisory board/legislative body approval for other home occupations.

Fifteen (55 percent) of the ordinances did not have any provisions relating to approval or registration requirements. Of those that did require formal approval (12 ordinances), seven used a staff approval mechanism; three used an advisory board/legislative body approval process; and two required licensing by another municipal department. It should be noted that none of the ordinances allowed some home occupations to operate "unregistered" while other home occupations in the community had to be registered; in other words, if a community employed a registration program, all home occupations had to be registered.

TABLE 9. ADMINISTRATIVE PROVISIONS

Types of limits	Number of ordinances containing this limit
No provisions	15
Registration/license	12
Staff approved	3
Board approved	9
By other department	2

A CRITIQUE OF HOME OCCUPATION REGULATIONS

The reader should take into consideration that these comments are coming from a current zoning administrator who formerly operated a home-based business. In some cases, it will be obvious that the comment originates from one of those perspectives. In other cases, the perspective might not be so obvious.

The "zoning administrator" comments originate from enforcement problems and citizen questions since 1972. They reflect the frustrations of administering and enforcing vague and poorly defined limitations and standards.

The other perspective comes from an artist creating acrylic paintings and hand-made paper, and a planning consultant. They reflect the desire for minimal regulations and clear, precise language of what I can and cannot do (and how I can do it).

At first glance, it may seem that the two perspectives would frequently be at odds with each other, but this is not necessarily the case. Eliminating flawed ordinance language can benefit the zoning professional and the home-based business operator. If business operators know exactly what

If the business operator and the zoning enforcement official can come together through a citizen participation process to identify and examine the flaws in the current regulations, the process of eliminating flawed language and vagueness might move more quickly and effectively.

the limits are on their business, they can often adjust their operations to comply with the ordinance and avoid problems with the local authorities. If the zoning professional has specific, measurable standards and limitations to enforce, accusations of unfair and uneven enforcement can be minimized or eliminated. Most importantly, if the business operator and the zoning enforcement official can come together through a citizen participation process to identify and examine the flaws in the current regulations, the process of eliminating flawed language and vagueness might move more quickly and effectively. The "buy-in" effect of receiving this input cannot be overestimated. Even if that input means the need for a total rewrite of the ordinance, that is better than struggling through the revision of a fundamentally flawed document.

Most of the comments here constitute criticism, but I will also note provisions and ordinance language that address these criticisms in innovative ways. Although these comments and criticisms are directed to the ordinances examined in this report, I believe they apply to home occupation regulations in general in that the ordinances examined were representative of the larger universe.

Zoning Ordinance Organization

My first comment addresses the overall organization of a zoning ordinance. Planners tend to fragment and scatter home-based business regulations throughout the zoning ordinance. The zoning regulations governing home occupations are often separated from those governing other business activities, such as garage sales, day care facilities, the renting of rooms, bed and breakfast inns, and the sale of agricultural products grown on the property. Only one of the "home occupation" regulations addressed garage sales, and only a few addressed day care facilities.

Although this may reflect a personal bias, I am inclined to believe that functional grouping of the zoning regulations makes the zoning ordinance more "citizen friendly" and easier to use. I also recognize that adopting an entirely new zoning ordinance is a relatively rare undertaking and reviewing other municipal codes for possible consolidations even more rare. These various regulations developed over time and for a variety of social, political, and economic reasons. Obviously, adding regulations that previously were in some other section of a municipal or county code to a zoning ordinance may make it a bit more complex and/or lengthy.

Telecommuting as a Home Occupation

The vast majority of the zoning ordinances do not address telecommuting or what the Bureau of Labor Statistics classifies as "unpaid work at home" (i.e., taking work home from the office). Zoning ordinances often define home occupations as self-contained business entities with the assumption that the home worker is not part of a larger business organization. The home occupation regulations I examined for this report severely limit the numbers of employees a home-based worker may have and, with one exception, do not address the idea that the home-based worker might be somebody's employee. That is a problem given the continuing changes in the American workplace. Many employers are beginning to understand the cost benefits of having some employees work in their own homes. According to IDC/Link Resources, a market research firm, there were 17 million paid telecommuters in 1998. Differentiating between "unpaid work at home" and "paid work at home" may be a useless effort. Christopher Hansen, president of the Home-Based Business Council, Inc., points out that there is no difference between a worker bringing work home and a student doing homework. He recommends focusing on the real issue—the number of employees working in a home.

I first started to notice citizen inquiries about telecommuting in the early 1990s. Conscientious citizens would call or visit the planning office and, although there were no apparent reasons for prohibiting the practice, the practice was, in fact, prohibited if the ordinance was strictly interpreted. The alternative was to tell them that the home occupation regulations did not apply to their situation and telecommuting was permitted.

As a professional planner, I was made uncomfortable by this situation. If the citizen read the ordinance carefully, they often came to the conclusion that telecommuting was not permitted. The fact that the ordinance was "telling" them something different than the staff was telling them does not raise their comfort level in zoning/planning and government in general. The Corona, California, ordinance I examined in my research for this report was the first zoning ordinance that I have ever seen in a 28-year career containing language that specifically permits telecommuting as a home occupation.

Differentiating between "unpaid work at home" and "paid work at home" may be a useless effort . . . there is no difference between a worker bringing work home and a student doing homework.

Differentiating between Types of Home Occupations

Planners often take a "one size fits all" approach to home occupation regulations. Few zoning ordinances differentiate between types of home-based business based on their activities or their "intensity" (e.g., type and amount of traffic generated). As is noted in the review of the legal treatises above, the courts have differentiated between a one-chair beauty salon with a couple of customers a day and a three-chair salon with employees and a substantial clientele. We may want to consider regulating different levels of business activity differently (i.e., some occupations should be permitted by right, some with staff approval and registration, and some with a public hearing/board approval).

Even fewer ordinances provide different home occupation regulations for different zoning district classifications. To some extent, the absence of different home occupation regulation for different zoning classifications may be attributed to a lack of diversity in residential zoning classifications. While I am not suggesting that there be different home occupation regulations for every residential zoning classification, I am suggesting that some consideration needs to be given to making such differentiations in jurisdictions that are marked by a variety of types of districts (e.g., an outlying suburb with both low-density residential, high-density residential, and agricultural areas).

Internet-based Businesses

Although some progress has been made, a surprisingly large number of home occupation regulations do not do a very good job with some of the new ways of conducting business. Steven King is experimenting with and exploring the possibilities of selling his books directly to the reader; namely, works he has written from his computer to your computer via the Internet. A number of musical groups are also experimenting with similar business models. Are they selling directly to the customer? Are they violating their local home occupation regulations? Problems in this area are often associated with how they handle sales and shipping, if any.

This area is further complicated by the less savory part of the Internet, the availability and sale of "adult" and "pornographic" material over the Internet. Dealing with this problem is like sitting on a wobbly, three-legged stool. The first leg is the problem of defining and regulating these materials; the second leg is the matter of the legislators and, subsequently, the courts, establishing laws relating to "where" Internet commerce takes place (e.g., is it the place of business or the site of the server?); and the third leg being how much a local government chooses to regulate "adult" uses.

Although none of the ordinances that I studied had provisions dealing with "adult" uses as a home occupation, it would seem likely that we will start to see them addressed more frequently in the future.

A recent case, *Voyeur Dorm L.C. v. City of Tampa* (Case No. 8:99-cv2180-T-24F (U.S. M. Dist. Fla. 2000)), showed some of the potential difficulties. Voyeur Dorm was a house in Tampa that offered 24-hour viewing of six "college-age" women for a fee. No one knew the nature of the business being conducted in the home until the business sought to register with the city. A judge finally decided in favor of the city by finding that Voyeur Dorm constituted an adult use and was, therefore, prohibited in the residential zone in which it was located.

Many home occupation regulations still contain language that can be interpreted in any number of ways. Such regulations can be the zoning administrator's ultimate nightmare.

Clearly, localities may need to examine both their adult use regulations and their home occupation regulations to avoid potential problems. In the first instance, the adult use regulations need to contain a definition that classifies such an operation as an adult use. In the home occupation regulations, the prohibited use list could "point" at the adult use definitions to describe prohibited home businesses. (For further information on this topic, see *Everything You Always Wanted to Know About Regulating Sex Businesses* by Eric Damian Kelly and Connie Cooper, PAS Report Nos. 495/496 (Chicago: APA, 2000))

Sales

Most of the ordinances had some limitations on sales. Some made distinctions between retail and wholesale sales that I question. Is there any more of an adverse impact on the surrounding neighbors of an artist having a collector come to the studio to purchase a sheet of hand-made paper than having a gallery owner come to purchase ten sheets of hand-made paper?

Number of Employees

Most of the home occupation ordinances prohibited or severely limited the number of employees that a home occupation could have. Only two of the ordinances differentiated between employees working in the residence and employees working in their own homes or at work locations elsewhere. I distinctly remember having to tell a resident who happened to be a medical supply exporter with five employees—none of them living or working in this country—that he was technically violating his community's zoning regulations. It was an all too familiar circumstance to then tell that resident that the city would ignore that particular provision. But that clearly left the business operator in a sticky situation—what if new staff felt differently in the future?

Such technical violations are the ones that most need close examination and clarification to avoid putting both the business operator and the zoning staff in such an awkward situation. Clearly, if the concern is the impact of the home-based business on the residential area, the number of employees actually working in the home is a clearer and simpler criterion for deciding what is and what is not a home-based business that is allowable in a residential zone.

Vague, Discretionary Standards

Many home occupation regulations still contain language that can be interpreted in any number of ways. Such regulations can be the zoning administrator's ultimate nightmare. Regulations addressing equipment, for example, often include provisions specifying that "equipment must be typical to a residence." How large of a percentage of residences must contain a particular piece of equipment before I consider it "typical"? In the early 1980s, a computer was a relatively rare thing to be found in a home. Was there any good reasoning for banning it as an element in a home occupation? With the wide variety of hobby and home repair equipment available today, I am even less sure about what is typical. This same kind of vagueness carries over into other aspects of regulating home-based businesses (e.g., "typical" traffic generation rates).

Many of the ordinances contain contradictions and, if enforced literally, unintended consequences. The Woodridge, Illinois, home occupation regulations are a good example of this phenomenon. The prohibited use list in that ordinance bars "manufacturing and processing of any kind." Does that mean no word processing? No data processing? Probably not, considering that their "permitted use list" contains typists.

The answer to this problem, like the one related to employees, is contained in the measurable impact of the home-based business activities on the area. Technology can work for the zoning staff in this case. More sophisticated equipment for measuring noise, vibration, emissions, and other byproducts of activity are available. Use of the equipment may require some training or hiring a consultant familiar with the equipment. The bottom line is that, with quantitative standards and measuring equipment, violations of the ordinance become clear and the need for (and difficulty of) getting access to a residence to do an in-house inspection is eliminated or can be triggered by clear evidence of a violation.

After giving a lot of thought to and taking several attempts at creating a "model" ordinance, I came to the conclusion that it is a task doomed to failure. It seemed highly unlikely that it could possibly result in a high-quality ordinance suitable for all jurisdictions . . .

SUGGESTIONS FOR GOVERNING HOME-BASED BUSINESS ACTIVITIES

After giving a lot of thought to and taking several attempts at creating a "model" ordinance, I came to the conclusion that it is a task doomed to failure. It seemed highly unlikely that it could possibly result in a high-quality ordinance suitable for all (rural, suburban, and urban) jurisdictions with wide varieties of staff sizes and expertise to administer and enforce it. The conclusion was also influenced by a career-long love/hate relationship with "model" ordinances. I have found that models often create more work for a planner than they are worth. Because they are called "models," one is tempted to follow them closely, but any good ordinance still needs to be "massaged" to address a community's characteristics, problems, past practices, and current politics. Add to that problems of formatting, different organization, and more, and I concluded a model would be less useful than a good series of recommendations.

So, I am not going to write a model ordinance, but I am providing a "how-to" manual. The first half of these instructions focuses on issues and decisions that will have to be addressed before you actually begin to draft ordinance language. The second half contains an ordinance framework, suggestions, and a full range of options to consider for regulating home-based business.

In the interest of full disclosure, I must admit to being an unabashed proponent of home-based businesses. I believe that the benefits of home-based businesses to our society far outweigh any of the minor negative impacts they may have on surrounding residences. They provide solutions to many of the most critical social, economic, and environmental problems facing our nation in the twenty-first century. They can:

- help us reduce the energy we consume getting to work;
- reduce the number of cars on our streets (particularly during peak hours);

It doesn't take a rocket scientist to figure out that, if something isn't working, you don't keep doing the same, exact thing over again in hopes that it will eventually work.

- serve as economic development tools or "incubators";
- provide parents with the opportunity to be more directly involved in the raising of their children (and avoiding the risks—medical, accidental, and criminal—sometimes associated with modern day care);
- provide the working poor a way to make ends meet without having to take on a second outside job that takes them from their family activities;
- provide the thousands of people that our corporations lay off every year with the means to stay financially solvent until they can find another job (or decide to abandon the corporate culture entirely and strike out on their own);
- minimize the overhead expenses of our businesses (and the number of acres of "sprawl" that we devote to office complexes); and
- nurture the development of new, innovative business models.

I also have no doubt that there are benefits that I have not mentioned and am not aware of.

I also believe that a significant portion of our home-based business regulations are useless at best and, in many cases, unwarranted, unnecessarily restrictive, and irrational. They are the type of zoning regulation that has damaged the credibility of the planning profession and why the courts have increasingly told planners that planners have gone too far. One could make the argument that our home occupation regulations are very class/economically biased, favoring the "professions" and upper-class endeavors while prohibiting the more blue-collar occupations, such as mechanics, repair, and construction trades.

As I mentioned above, I will try to give you a fairly complete range of options in use today. That does not mean that I believe that all these options are good and/or should be used. On the contrary, I would consider many of them to fall in the class of regulations referred to in the first sentence of this paragraph. I will let you know what I think about a lot of these regulations, concentrating my "editorializing" in the Commentary sections.

The thing that I found most striking about the last two PAS Reports on home occupation regulation is that they identified the same problems that we are talking about today. In many respects, the regulations presented were not significantly different from those mentioned in the first PAS Report on this subject. It doesn't take a rocket scientist to figure out that, if something isn't working, you don't keep doing the same, exact thing over again in hopes that it will eventually work. Even a chimpanzee will give up on trying to put a square peg into a round hole after a couple of tries.

Now that I have you all fired up to bring some radical twenty-first century thinking to your zoning ordinance, I am also going to tell to be VERY CAREFUL. Introducing radical ideas and new ways of thinking about things can be a very dangerous professional undertaking. Although this warning is mostly for the younger planners out there, the more "seasoned" planners should not discount it. It is like working with a live 220-volt line in a wet basement (and this warning is coming from somebody who had his eyebrows and moustache severely singed earlier this year). There is a very real potential that your supervisor will think you're a total wash out, your staff may "revolt," you could have a Plan Commission Chair turn to you (after they reject your ideas) and say, "Old is better."

The business community won't necessarily support your ideas as some of the more traditional "Main Street" businesses may view home-based businesses as a threat.

The first task in revising your home-based business regulations is to formulate an overall strategy for your regulatory efforts. This task will be heavily dependant on the nature of your undertaking and the answer to the question, What is the government's objective in regulating home-based businesses? It seems imperative that you need to talk with the home-based business industry as early as possible to help you critique your current regulations. The contacts you make during this phase will also be valuable later when developing specific ordinance language. Some approaches may be more appropriate for total zoning ordinance replacements and others for a more surgical "fix" of your current home occupation regulations.

If you are addressing a few minor problems in your existing ordinance, a few small modifications may be all that is needed. It seems that a couple of minor changes in most current home occupation regulations would go a long way to legalize a great number of home-based businesses and business activities that, technically, do not comply with your home occupation regulations but do not cause any problems or generate neighborhood complaints.

If you are creating an entirely new zoning ordinance or have decided that a complete revision of the home occupation regulations is warranted, the options available to you will, in all likelihood, be more numerous. One might consider a very inclusive set of home-based business regulations. Many communities have provisions regulating day care centers and garage sales, and they may or may not be in the zoning ordinance and may or may not be in the zoning ordinance's home occupation regulations. It may make sense to consolidate all the regulations relating to home-based business activities in one section of the zoning ordinance.

As I mentioned above, an effort should not be undertaken without getting input from the people you will be regulating. Their advice and suggestions can be invaluable. It may be difficult drawing them "out in the open." Perhaps an informal announced meeting in which the planning staff "guarantees" the anonymity of attendants will be preserved (e.g., no sign-in sheet, recording of comments without attribution or only with agreement that attribution can be recorded, etc.) would work well or at least get the ball rolling. If all else fails, you may want to talk to some home-based business operators outside of your jurisdiction (i.e., those that have no worry that you will use this information in any enforcement actions).

Another important consideration is the nature of the jurisdiction. A high-density urban jurisdiction's needs are very different from an agricultural county's needs. Jurisdictions with wide varieties of residential zoning district types may justify a more sophisticated set of regulations. The size of the jurisdiction will also likely have impacts on the size and expertise of the staff available to administer and enforce the zoning ordinance. This consideration may also be affected by the local community's attitude toward "regulation" in general.

A close examination of past practices, both in terms of what has been allowed and what has been prohibited, seems advisable. Complaints about home-based business activities are an important source of information about what causes complaints in terms of specific uses and business practices. You may want to investigate to see if there are large numbers of technically illegal home-based businesses that do not generate problems or complaints. Looking through the yellow pages, newspaper ads, and bulletin boards in local businesses will give you a pretty good idea of what businesses are out there.

A high-density urban jurisdiction's needs are very different from an agricultural county's needs. Jurisdictions with wide varieties of residential zoning district types may justify a more sophisticated set of regulations.

Another strategic decision that needs to be made focuses on the question of stratification; namely, should the community differentiate between types of home occupations and the provisions that apply to each type? Although the concept of regulatory stratification introduces a significant complexity and length to the regulations, it may be a valuable tool if you are interested in developing more permissive regulations. If that approach is being used, you may want to allow some business activities in the home by right and without registration (e.g., the telecommuters, home offices), some requiring staff approval and registration, and some that require a public hearing and advisory/legislative body approval and registration.

There is also the question of having different home-based business regulations in the different zoning districts. Considering the large numbers of agricultural and residential zoning district types, having individual home-based business regulations for each zoning district could easily get out of hand. I believe that most jurisdictions can get by with two, or at most, three "sets" of home-based business regulations. Creating regulations that differentiate between home-based businesses in agricultural districts, residential districts, and then further to single-family or multifamily residential districts would probably be adequate in most cases. A community dominated by low-density, single-family residential development probably doesn't need to consider multiple sets of home-based business regulations.

The provisions that are most likely to be employed in stratification are the administrative provisions and the lists of permitted and prohibited uses. I provide some suggestions below.

Many of the factors discussed previously have a very direct relation to how complex, long, and sophisticated your home-based business regulations will be. They have direct implications for how complicated you want your home-based business regulations to be and how complicated they need to be. Parts of both the zoning administrator and home-based business operator would like short, concise, easily understood and enforced regulations. At the same time, both of these groups may want a more permissive ordinance, which seems to lead to a more complicated, lengthy set of regulations. There is no one correct approach. Finding that acceptable compromise is likely to be as much of an art as a science.

I would like to present one last idea that you may want to consider. It may be time to abandon the concept of and term "home occupation." To me, it is too closely tied to Bassett's version of the traditional home occupation consisting of the "professions." It comes with too much limiting legal "baggage" in inconsistent court decisions and interpretations. Over the years, most zoning ordinances have significantly expanded the numbers and types of business activities allowed in the residence. I would suggest that is time to call these activities what they are, home-based businesses.

The framework I suggest for organizing home-based business regulations follows. The principal sections are:

Definitions

I. Intent/purpose

II. Administration

III. Permitted Home-Based Businesses

IV. Prohibited Home-Based Businesses

V. Operational Standards

Definitions

This may be a personal preference, but I prefer putting the definitions in a definitions section rather than in the subject area regulations. I am also of the belief that the definition should not be the mechanism to limit home-based business activities; namely, definitions should not contain regulatory standards. Finally, definitions should be relatively simple and short.

> ***Home-based business:*** Any business, occupation, or activity undertaken for gain within a residential structure that is incidental and secondary to the use of that structure as a dwelling unit.

I have also included a second definition if the reader is inclined to have a two-tiered system of home-based businesses/business activities.

> ***Home office:*** An accessory use in which work for compensation is undertaken, including, but not limited to, receiving or initiating correspondence, such as phone calls, mail, faxes, or e-mail; preparing or maintaining business records; word and data processing; and telephone, mail order, and off-premise sales.

Definitions should not contain regulatory standards. . . . Definitions should be relatively simple and short.

I. Intent/Purpose

The following language should provide a good starting point for developing an Intent Section:

> The [city/county] recognizes the desire and/or need of some citizens to use their residence for business activities in order to reduce trip generation and to provide another economic development tool, but [it] also recognizes the need to protect the surrounding areas from adverse impacts generated by these business activities.

Commentary: *A separate Intent Section in the ordinance may not be necessary, particularly if the definition includes language specifically addressing the intention of the regulations. I would suggest that, if you are doing something innovative or different than usual, you may want to include a separate Intent section. This would give the courts a little more information about what your jurisdiction is trying to do in the event that your home-based business regulations are challenged in the courts.*

II. Administration

Registering or licensing. This is one of the sections that can be used to introduce another element of stratification if desired. If registration or licensing is going to be required, this is a logical place for it to be. References to other licensing or code requirements (e.g., health department regulations, fire and safety codes, and separate business licenses) may also be included here. The next decision involves determining who will review and approve the applications for a home business license. This can involve a staff approval and/or registration/licensing, a public hearing process, and advisory board/legislative body approval or some combination of the two.

Commentary: *I am not a big proponent of registering/licensing home-based business. Part of my reluctance comes from my belief that, as professional planners, we have a lot more important if not critical things to deal with than filling out forms on home-based businesses. For some unknown, cosmic reason, applicants always come in when you are trying to get seven agenda/staff reports off to the planning commission or getting ready for a big presentation to the city council. At the very least, I would try to severely minimize the number of home-based businesses that you have to register to reduce your administrative costs.*

I would suggest that you not require registration/licensing of any home offices or home-based businesses that do not have customer/client visits, on-premise employees, a commercial vehicle (exceeding 3/4 ton), and trailer/equipment storage. If your jurisdiction licenses traditional "Main Street" businesses through a different department (such as a Clerk's office), it makes no sense to maintain or establish a separate system for licensing home-based businesses in the Planning Department.

Any licensing fees should reflect the actual administrative costs of issuing the licenses rather than as an additional revenue generator. Although many businesses may resent the licensing requirement, if it is a minimal fee and easy to do, they may consider it acceptable and a means to build up their business's credibility/legitimacy, a problem many beginning businesses face.

The downside to not registering/licensing home-based business is that we will hamstring any attempts to do any rigorous study of the impacts of home-based businesses on our communities. We need good information about the number of home-based businesses and their location. I would not be surprised at all that a thorough analysis might reveal that there are a variety of quantifiable benefits to our communities, and I always wished I had some hard data to help me push for more permissive regulations.

The downside to not registering/licensing home-based business is that we will hamstring any attempts to do any rigorous study of the impacts of home-based businesses on our communities. We need good information about the number of home-based businesses and their location.

License renewals and inspections. If a jurisdiction is inclined to have some sort of registration or licensing provisions, you may want to consider requiring an annual renewal. The fact is that a large percentage of start-up businesses go out of business in the first few years. Removing those businesses from your databases enables you to have accurate, up-to-date information to use when making policy decisions. Recently, some ordinances have included language requiring that the home-based business give the community the right to inspect the property for compliance with the home-based business regulations.

Commentary: *The "inspection" issue is another problematic area, both in the initial approval and enforcement activities. If you are inclined to include provisions requiring the right to inspect for compliance, I would strongly recommend some "standards" for the justification of an enforcement inspection (e.g., a neighbor or customer complaint, an advertisement of a prohibited activity, or the off-premise observation of a prohibited activity or condition). You may want to consult your attorneys on the "standards" for search warrants for their use as a guide. I am not convinced that these provisions are necessary.*

Some agencies also conduct an initial inspection before issuing a permit or license. As a zoning administrator, I have always thought they were a waste of time and administrative resources. If home-based business operators are going to be zoning "outlaws," they will change everything to the way it works for their business after they get their license. I will discuss some other problems in this area in my Commentary in the "Use of Residence" section below.

Inspections would give the jurisdiction a much better idea of the number and location of home-based businesses in the community. The inspection right would also be of benefit to the enforcement staff in the event that the home-based business generates neighborhood complaints. Registration is your proverbial two-edged sword. It involves additional administrative responsibilities and effort for the city and, sometimes, expense for the business operator. It is also a great source of information on home-based business activities that can be invaluable in improving your home-based business regulations in the future.

Commentary: *I believe that having some business activities as a use by right without registration and some with staff approval merits serious consideration, particularly if you are consciously trying to be as inclusive as possible without adversely affecting the surrounding residential uses. The obvious shortcoming is that it introduces a significant complexity to the home-based business regulations.*

Enforcement. If no registration or licensing is going to be required and the zoning ordinance covers enforcement procedures and processes elsewhere, an administrative/enforcement section may not be necessary. For the purposes of illustration, I am including language that creates a system with both staff-approved and advisory body approved home-based businesses.

Commentary: *For the purposes of illustration, I have chosen to use a two-tiered system. Take it as an example rather than a recommendation. A logical break or division point for a two-tiered system would seem to be those home-based businesses with no or very limited customer/employee visits and those having more frequent and/or long stays by customers/employees. Other businesses with the potential to generate problems may warrant inclusion on the second list. Obviously, if you choose not to register/license home-based businesses, you will not need the following language.*

> No Level-1 home-based business shall be conducted until an application for a Level-1 Home-Based Business Permit has been reviewed and approved by the Zoning Administrator or his/her designee. The application shall include the following:
>
> 1. The address of the property
> 2. The resident's name
> 3. The owner's name (if different than resident)
> 4. The type of business and business activities
> 5. The number of employees
> 6. The location and area of the home-based business
> 7. The vehicles used in the home-based business
> 8. The number of expected customer visits per day and at any onetime.
>
> The Zoning Administrator shall issue the Home-based Business Permit or provide the applicant reasons for denial in the event that the application is not approved within three business days. The applicant may appeal the Zoning Administrator's decision to deny a Home-Based Business Permit to the Zoning Board of Appeals.
>
> The Home-Based Business Permit is valid for a one-year period and must be renewed if the residence continues to be used for business activities. The Zoning Administrator has the right to inspect the home-based business and premises to check for compliance with the home-based business regulations.
>
> No Level-2 home-based business shall be conducted until the applicant has completed an application showing the following information:
>
> 1. The address of the property
> 2. The resident's name
> 3. The owner's name (if different than resident)
> 4. The type of business and business activities
> 5. The number of employees
> 6. The location and area of the home-based business
> 7. The vehicles used in the home-based business
> 8. The number of expected customer visits per day
>
> The Zoning Board of Appeals shall conduct a Public Hearing on the application and approve or deny the Level-2 Home-Based Business Permit.
>
> The Level-2 Home-Based Business Permit is valid for a one-year period and must be renewed if the home-based business continues to operate. The Zoning Administrator has the right to inspect the home-based business and premises to check for compliance with the home-based business regulations.

If no registration or licensing is going to be required and the zoning ordinance covers enforcement procedures and processes elsewhere, an administrative/enforcement section may not be necessary.

Fees for the Home-Based Business Permits shall be specified in the (city/county) Schedule of Fees and Charges

or

Fees for the Home-Based Business Permits shall be:

Level-1 Home-based Business Permit..................................$X

Level-2 Home-based Business Permit..................................$Y

Commentary: *The ordinance language that I have provided has been influenced by two factors, a personal bias toward extremely permissive home-based business regulations and an effort to be as inclusive as possible to illustrate a variety of possibilities. A governmental entity may choose to take a different approach than my suggestion. One final suggestion— if you decide to register/license home-based businesses, put your application form on a web page (along with all your other application forms). Its just plain, good customer service and minimizes the use of paper.*

If you are preparing regulations for an Agricultural Zoning District, you may want to allow some business activities outside of the structures.

Use of the residence. At first glance, it would appear that the only decision would be whether to limit the business activity to the principal residential structure or the principal and accessory structures. If a more a more restrictive approach is desired, limiting it to a room, a specific percentage of the structure's area, or a specific maximum area can be used. If a percentage of the structure's area is used, 15 to 30 percent was the range that appeared most often in the ordinances I examined. A lower percentage may be more appropriate for higher-density zoning districts if a stratified approach is going to be used. The upper ranges of the percentage limits may make sense for lower-density residential and agricultural zoning districts.

Commentary: *I have always considered this a problematic area. One of the problems is that people today, if not in the past, use a number of rooms for short periods of time in which they work. In my professional artist days, I had a permanent area set up for doing large (4'x8') paintings in what had been a dining room. But for a couple hours every week, I would sit on the living room with a drawing board on my lap and do charcoal or ink drawings. Once every other week, the kitchen became a papermaking studio for an afternoon. With the advent of the laptop and palm computers, we, no doubt, have people wandering all over the house and yard "conducting business," and many may have no one permanent room or spot where they conduct business.*

Another of the problems is the use of accessory structures. I have always found ordinances prohibiting "home occupations" from accessory structures and requiring that commercial vehicles be stored in garages to be a strange mix of puzzling and amusing. I am a firm believer that home-based businesses should be permitted in accessory structures as long as they comply with the other performance standards. The first Apple Computers were made in Steve Job's garage. I have no idea what the home occupation regulations were in 1976 in that community, so I can't tell you if he was a "zoning outlaw." I don't want to be the planner that shuts down this century's Apple Computers.

The following language should be suitable for use in zoning district types where you want to severely limit the exterior use of the premises:

The home-based business must be conducted within the principal residential structure and permitted accessory structures, and shall not use more than 25 percent of the gross floor area of the structures.

If you are preparing regulations for an Agricultural Zoning District, you may want to allow some business activities outside of the structures. The following language would be suitable for these situations:

> The home-based business may be conducted within and outside of the residence and accessory structures. The home-based business interior activities shall not use more than 25 percent of the total gross floor area of these structures and not more than 10 percent of the lot area for exterior business activities.

Commentary: *There is nothing sacrosanct about the numbers I have used in the suggested language. I would not hesitate in adjusting them up or down to fit a local need.*

III. Permitted Home-Based Businesses

This section of your regulations is probably the heart of your home-based business regulations. The question of using Permitted Use and Prohibited Use Lists or a performance standards system in home occupation regulations has been debated since the early 1950s. As is often the case, each has its strengths and weaknesses. The list approach gives the administrator and the citizen a definitive set of uses that may or may not be permitted, a definite plus. The weakness of this approach is the likelihood that the lists will become outdated soon and/or that they were not very complete or comprehensive to begin with. A performance-based system offers the advantages of maximizing flexibility and adaptability to a changing business world. It is, however, more difficult to write and more difficult and costly to administer.

A hybrid approach may offer a third alternative. There seems to be some movement to using generalized, inclusive lists of permitted businesses along with some relatively simple performance standards. This approach may give the flexibility and adaptability of the performance-based approach while providing some of the certainty of the list approach.

There seems to be some movement to using generalized, inclusive lists of permitted businesses along with some relatively simple performance standards. This approach may give the flexibility and adaptability of the performance-based approach while providing some of the certainty of the list approach.

There are a number of options available if a stratified approach is going to be used. It may make sense to have different permitted and conditionally permitted lists for different zoning classifications. I am not suggesting that you need a different list for each zoning district. I would think that two or three lists should suffice in most situations. Lists for agricultural districts, detached single-family residential districts, and medium- to high-density residential districts seem appropriate.

Some home-based businesses that would clearly be problematic in a residential zoning district may not cause any problems in an agricultural district. Kennels and stables are the first that come to mind, but others could include equipment and vehicle repair, welding, and trucking. Permitted use lists for high-density urban zoning districts would likely be more restrictive than those used in the other districts.

Another technique to stratify your ordinance would be to permit some uses with a staff approval and others with a public hearing process and advisory and/or legislative body approval. A similar approach would be to allow some as a use by right and some with a staff approval and registration. The two could be combined to produce a three-tiered approach.

Commentary: *A number of previously cited publications and ordinances have generalized lists of permitted uses, and I will also follow that course. It relies heavily on the ideas suggested by Michael Frank in his* Planning *story (June 1993), with some additions I have gleaned from various ordinances. I have attempted to be as inclusive as possible.*

> Permitted Home-Based Businesses
>
> 1. Offices for such professionals as, but not limited to, architects, brokers, counselors, clergy, dentists, doctors, draftspersons and cartographers, engineers, insurance agents, lawyers, real estate agents, accountants, editors, publishers, journalists, psychologists, contract management, graphic design, construction contractors, landscape design, surveyors, cleaning services, salespersons and manufacturer's representatives, travel agents

2. Personal services, including barbershops, beauty parlors, manicure and pedicure shops, pet grooming, catering and chauffeuring services
3. Instructional services, including music, dance, art and craft classes, and tutoring
4. Babysitting services, day care homes
5. Studios for artists, sculptors, musicians, photographers, and authors
6. Workrooms for tailors, dressmakers, milliners, and craft persons, including weaving, lapidary, jewelry making, cabinetry and woodworking
7. Repair services, including watch and clocks, small appliances, computers, electronic devices, lawnmowers, and small engines
8. Rooming and boarding houses, bed & breakfast facilities
9. Garage/yard sales, "tupperware" parties

It is recognized that this list may not totally inclusive. The Zoning Administrator shall make the determination of whether an unlisted business is similar to a listed permitted use and issue or deny a Home-Based Business Permit.

A list of prohibited home-based businesses may not be necessary, or it may simply consist of a statement prohibiting anything not on the permitted home-based businesses list.

IV. Prohibited Home-Based Businesses

A list of prohibited home-based businesses may not be necessary, or it may simply consist of a statement prohibiting anything not on the permitted home-based businesses list. If you are considering limits on, or the prohibition of, some types of sales, including them in the prohibited use list makes sense and might be clearer than putting the limit or prohibition in provisions addressing operational limits.

Again, if a stratified approach is being considered, you will probably want to think about different prohibited use lists for different zoning districts. It certainly seems likely that some home-based businesses prohibited in a suburban or urban setting may be suitable in a rural area. Likewise, a list of prohibited home-based businesses for a high-density urban area may be more extensive and inclusive.

The following list contains uses that are commonly prohibited as home occupations in a suburban or urban setting. As I did in the list of permitted home-based businesses, I have tried to be as inclusive as possible. Some home-based businesses will appear on both lists for the purpose of illustration.

Prohibited home-based businesses

1. Kennels, stables, veterinarian clinics/hospitals
2. Medical and dental clinics, hospitals
3. Restaurants, clubs, drinking establishments
4. Motor vehicle/small engine repair
5. Barbershops/beauty salons
6. Undertaking and funeral parlors
7. Retail sales of goods not made on the premises
8. Adult uses

V. Operational Standards

Limits on operating hours. The provisions governing customer/client visits and deliveries are highly dependent on the types of home-based business activities allowed. If the permitted use list is very restrictive, separate provisions limiting customer/client visits may not be necessary. Where a jurisdiction wants to take a more permissive approach, I would suggest some limit on the quantity and/or intensity of customer visits and deliveries, and the hours in which they occur, to protect the surrounding residential area

Commentary: *A jurisdiction should probably consider a combination of limitations on customer visitation. There are three areas where customer visits can generate negative impacts on the surrounding residences. The first is the time of day that they visit the residence. The second is the total number of customer visits to the residence in a day. Third is the total number of customers that can be present at any one time. An 8:00 A.M. to 6:00 or 8:00 P.M. limitation on customer visits is probably suitable for most jurisdictions. The number of customer visits can be limited to a few (1 to 3) at any one time and to a total daily limit (4 to 10). There is nothing sacrosanct about these particular numbers or times. I wouldn't hesitate to adjust them to fit a local norm.*

Some exceptions to provisions governing the time and number of customer visits may need to be addressed. This is particularly the case if one has inclusive home-based business regulations covering such uses as day care facilities, garage sales, "tupperware" parties, and boarding, rooming, or bed and breakfast facilities. This may also be an appropriate place to include class-size limitations for instructional uses.

> Customer/client visits to the home-based business are limited to the hours from 9 A.M. to 8 P.M. The home-based business shall not generate more than 10 customer/client visits in any one day and no more than five customers/clients can be present at any one time.

Employees. I would suggest that your provisions address the issues of on-premise and off-premise employees. The home-based business proponent side of me would advise that employees working at locations other than at the residence of the business operator should be permitted. The zoning administrator in me hasn't been able to discern any negative impacts on the surrounding residences if employees are not regularly on the premises.

Commentary: *The Woodridge, Illinois, home occupation regulations provide us with a very simple and easy way to address this problem. They simply inserted "on-premise" in front of employees in their employee regulations. Separate on-premise and off-premise employee provisions should be considered if any specific limitations or conditions for off-premise employees are warranted.*

If a total rewrite or new home occupation regulations are in order or if you want a very simple, brief, yet efficient regulation, you may want to consider combining the on-premise employee provisions with the customer/client limitations. This may be a gross generalization, but most home occupation regulations are more permissive when it comes to customer/client visits than to on-premise employees. I have some serious doubts that these differences are merited. As a zoning administrator in an enforcement mode, I do not have to establish or determine a function of a business visit.

> The home-based business shall have no more than one nonresident employee on the premises at any one time. The number of nonresident employees working at locations other than the home-based business is not limited.

Vehicles. I would group all of the vehicular restrictions in one functional area. If you want to cover all the bases you will want to consider three areas:

- commercial vehicles owned and used by the home-based business;

Some exceptions to provisions governing the time and number of customer visits may need to be addressed. This is particularly the case if one has inclusive home-based business regulations covering such uses as day care facilities, garage sales, "tupperware" parties, and boarding, rooming, or bed and breakfast facilities.

- the vehicles (and times) used to deliver goods to the home-based business; and
- the vehicles used by the customer/clients and employees.

If you choose to prohibit certain types of delivery vehicles, you may want to use your state's vehicle classification system to determine the cut-off for vehicle size.

Limits on the number, type, and hours that deliveries can be made can be used to protect the surrounding residences. Most ordinances allow deliveries by passenger vehicles, mail carriers and, more frequently, they are including step vans (i.e., the type of truck commonly used by United Parcel Service and Federal Express). If you choose to prohibit certain types of delivery vehicles, you may want to use your state's vehicle classification system to determine the cut-off for vehicle size. If you opt to limit delivery hours, an 8:00 A.M. to 6:00 P.M. range may be appropriate.

A closely related issue is the regulation of commercial vehicles owned and used by the home-based business. It seems that limitations on the number of vehicles, their size and type, and the location of their parking and storage may be considered necessary. Typically, ordinances limit the number of commercial vehicles to one, and many include a one-ton weight limit. Again, you may want to take a look at your state vehicle registration classification system for some help in developing your own limits. If you are going to require commercial vehicles to be stored in garages, you should check to see that your limits on the area of the property in which a home-based business is allowed to operate includes accessory structures for that purpose. If commercial vehicles are allowed to be stored outside, you may want to consider limiting them to a side or rear yard with some type of screening.

Commentary: *I am not entirely convinced that limits on visiting customer/client parking are necessary. This probably more likely to be true if the permitted use list effectively limits the number of people coming to the home-based business. In ordinances that are more permissive, some additional restrictions may be warranted. Many communities require hard-surfaced parking areas located outside of front and side yard setbacks.*

The following language may be used in this subject area:

> Delivery vehicles used to deliver goods to the home-based business are limited to passenger vehicles, mail carriers, and express carriers such as UPS. Deliveries shall be permitted between 8:00 A.M. and 6:00 P.M.
>
> The home-based business shall be limited to the parking/storage of one commercial vehicle on the premises, not exceeding a one-ton capacity.
>
> Level-1 Home-Based Businesses are not required to provide any additional parking beyond what is required for the residential use. Level-2 Home-Based Businesses shall provide two, hard, dust-free parking areas located outside of the front and side yard area.

Commentary: *I have used "two" rather arbitrarily, more as an example than a recommendation. The point being that the number of required parking spaces needs to be based on the maximum amount of traffic permitted. It should also be noted that ordinances with more than two levels of permits/permitting procedures may want to have more than two levels of parking requirements.*

Limits on equipment and operation "nuisances." Many ordinances have separate provisions addressing equipment and nuisance generation in the form of noise, odor, smoke, vibrations, light, electrical or communication device interference, etc. As noted above, using vague, discretionary terms like "typical" when describing the type of equipment that will be allowed will not do. I believe that a better approach is to combine the limitations of the home-based business operations and equipment. If you are inclined to use specific, measurable standards such as decibel limits/durations, I would suggest that any restrictions be limited to equipment that does not exceed any of the operational standards (i.e., the noise, smoke, vibrations and electrical interference).

Limitations on the storage and use of hazardous materials in home-based businesses present some problems for the zoning administrator. In consultation with a number of local and state fire marshals, I learned that this remains a vexing problem for them. The average single-family residence contains a variety of hazardous, toxic, flammable, and explosive materials. The mixture of a variety of relatively "safe" materials may result in dangerous substances and devices. The potentially dangerous materials can range from a gas can for the lawnmower to pesticides and cleaning materials. It appears that the quantity of hazardous materials, the ways they are stored and how they are used are all important factors. All three factors should be used in formulating specific, measurable limits on the storage and use of various hazardous materials. I would warn against using such provisions unless there is legitimate concern that some of the home occupations that a community includes on its permitted list of home occupations would, in fact, employ the use of a dangerous amount of hazardous materials. Otherwise, such provisions simply add to the length and complexity of the regulations.

The following language should be adequate in most situations.

> The equipment used by the home-based business and the operation of the home-based business shall not create any vibrations, heat, glare, dust, odors, or smoke discernable at the property lines, generate noise exceeding 60 decibels at the property line from 8:00 A.M. to 7:00 P.M., generate any noise discernable by the human ear at the property lines from 7:00 P.M. to 8:00 A.M., create any electrical, magnetic or other interference off the premises, consume utility quantities that negatively impact the delivery of those utilities to surrounding properties, or use and/or store hazardous materials in excess of quantities permitted in residential structures.

Commentary: *Again, the numbers and times used are provided as examples, not recommendations. If your community already has noise generation regulations, you may already have the measurable standard (and the equipment/personnel)to monitor compliance.*

I would strongly recommend talking to someone in the local fire and police departments about developing some relatively specific limits on the various types of hazardous materials. At the very least, these limits could be used by all city departments in an informally adopted policy. A more formal approval would result from their inclusion in this section of the ordinance. To a great extent, the limits will be affected by the residential building types/densities, the available equipment, training, water supply, and response times of the local departments. You may want to consider having limitations for flammables, explosives, toxins, as well as a list of banned materials, such as dynamite.

WUNDER RULES

If you are still with me, you may be feeling a bit overwhelmed. You thought "fixing the home occupation stuff" would be a quick, easy, maybe even fun task. Suddenly, the task may have become larger, more complex, time-consuming, and difficult than you thought it would be. Amending zoning ordinances can often have a "ripple" effect. The change of a word or phrase in one section of an ordinance may need to be made in other sections of the ordinance as well. The task doesn't necessarily have to become complex and, even if it does, the complexity can be managed.

The key is deciding what is needed and wanted in a particular jurisdiction. To a great extent, that may be determined by how well the current ordinance is functioning. Over my long career, I have come up with a set of "rules" that I use to evaluate existing ordinances and write new ones. I make no claim to being the creator of all of these rules. Most come from former supervisors, popular culture, and some respected notables, such as Eric Kelly. Obviously, some of these are offered tongue-in-cheek, but they should be taken just as seriously. They come with some commentary, but for the most part, should be self-explanatory.

1. **Don't forget that you (or a co-worker) will have to explain, administer, and enforce these regulations.**

   This one shouldn't need much explanation or clarification. If you have too much time on your hands, too little work to do, and not enough problems in your career, you can ignore this rule.

2. **Don't try to do too much with too little.**

   Watch the use of too many generalities and subjective terms in an effort to keep the regulations short and simple. Specific and measurable standards will mean more extensive regulations. If your objective is to develop a more permissive ordinance or if you have significantly different residential zoning districts, you need to seriously consider some stratification in your ordinance.

3. **Don't try to cover every variation of every conceivable type of home-based business.**

   Breaking this rule can result in a 400-page zoning ordinance with 200 pages of home-based business regulations. I can't believe that is what you need or want. There is a serious danger that this would in all likelihood cause more problems than it solves.

4. **Don't try to make it too complicated.**

   Closely related to Rules #1 and #3, but important enough to repeat again.

5. **Don't be afraid of using somebody else's good idea.**

   You have probably heard the cliché, "Don't reinvent the wheel." It became a cliché because it is such good advice. Following this rule may require a little more work, but with the number of zoning ordinances available on the Internet or with the assistance of the Planning Advisory Service, it is much easier than it used to be.

6. **Don't be afraid of doing something different, innovative, or creative.**

   Use this rule if Rule #5 doesn't work for you. If you have a problem or situation unique to your community, you may need to develop a unique solution to that problem or situation.

7. **Don't forget that the individual components of your regulations should work together.**

   When working on the language for specific provisions within your home-based business regulations, don't lose sight of the fact that these regulations exist within the context of a much larger set of regulations, your zoning ordinance.

8. **a) Say what you mean.**

   b) Mean what you say.

   This is one of the most important of the Wunder Rules and the only one with two components. You have undoubtedly heard this one before, but it says it so well.

9. **Write your regulations as if you have to administer and enforce them, especially if you aren't the one administering and enforcing them.**

   If you work in a two- or three-person office, you will have to do this, and I would question your intelligence or mental health if you want to make your job harder.

10. **This isn't brain surgery; if you don't get it right the first time, the world will not come to an end, and you can always take another shot at it.**

    If you create the perfect home-based business regulations, you won't have to worry about this rule, but please send me a copy of those regulations..

WHERE DO WE GO FROM HERE?

It seems likely that the ways of doing business will continue to evolve. I am not about to make myself look foolish by trying to tell you what the future will bring. I am probably the wrong person to ask. Ask a 15 year old. But I will tell you that it will continue to change. Some of these changes will undoubtedly affect and change the business activities in the home.

Just as there may be localized and regional differences in attitudes toward home-based businesses, it seems likely that these attitudes may change over time. It may be too early to see if neotraditional residential development becomes a dominant prototype, but if it does, it may be a forerunner of changing attitudes toward home-based businesses as well.

Currently, our ability to measure the impacts of home-based businesses is sketchy at best. Data from registrations and licensing will help, as will Geographic Information System databases that include thorough and accurate business information. I have to believe that more accurate information on the impact of home-based businesses on residential property values, vacancy rates, business incubation, and commercial vacancy rates will enable us to make better policy choices in regards to the magnitude of business activities we allow in residential neighborhoods.

So, it looks like we are destined to make incremental adjustments to our home-based business regulations into the future.

I have to believe that more accurate information on the impact of home-based businesses on residential property values, vacancy rates, business incubation, and commercial vacancy rates will enable us to make better policy choices in regards to the magnitude of business activities we allow in residential neighborhoods.

END NOTES

1. *Keller v. Westfield*, 39 NJ Super 430, 121 A2d 419 (1956); *Gratten v. Pellegrino*, 115 NH 619,348 A2d 349 (1975); *Maurer v. Snyder*, 199 Md 551, 87 A2d 612 (1952); *Muskegon Heights v. Wilson*, 163 Mich 263, 109 NW2d 768 (1961); *Perron v. City of Concord*, 102 NH 32, 150 A2d 403 (1959); *Mahler v. Bd. Of Adj.*, 94 NJ Super 173, 227nA2d 311 (1967) *aff'd* 55 NJ 1, 258 A2d 705 (1969); *Cauvel v. City of Tulsa*, 368 P2d 660 (Okla. 1962); *Lemp v. Milburn Twp.*, 129 NJL 221, 28 A2d 767 (1942); *Bourke v. Foster*, 343 SW2d 208 (Mo App 1960)

2. *City of Harrison v. Wilson*, 248 Ark. 736, 453 SW2d 730 (1970); *Jones v. Bd. Of Adj.*, 119 Colo. 420, 204 P2d 560 (1949), and *Red Acres Improve. Club, Inc. v. Burkhalter*, 193 Tenn. 79, 241 SW2d 921 (1951).

3. *Parish of Jefferson v. Groetsch*, 256 So2d 722 (La App) *cert denied* 260 La 1204,258 So2d 552 (1972) and *State v. Bandler*, 334 So2d 197 (La 1976).

4. *Commissioners of Belefonte v. Coppola*, 453 A2d 457 (Del. 1982) and *Parks v. Board of Adjustment,* 556 S.W.2d 365 (Tx. Civ. App.), *rehearing denied* (1978).

5. *Norton v. Lay*, 360 So.2d 239 (La.App. 1978); *Town of Kittery v. Hoyt*, 291 A2d 512 (Me. 1972); *Narbonne v. Town of Rye*, 1300 N.H. 70, 534 A2d 388 (1987); *Ames v. Palma*, 52 A.D.2d 1078, 384 N.Y.S.2d 587 (1976); *Grendal v. White*, 41 A.D.2d 887, 342 N.Y.S.2d 802 (1973); *Bobinson v. Ray*, 637 P2d 108 (Okla. 1981); *City of Florence v. Turboville,* 239 S,C. 126, 121S.E.2d 437 (1961) and *Boreth v. Philadelphia Bd. Of Adjustment*, 396 Pa. 82, 151 A2d 474 (1959).

6. *Fox v. Zoning Bd. of Appeals*, 146 Conn. 70, 147 A2d 472 (1958); *Metropolitan Dev. Comm'n v. Mullin*, 399 N.E.2d 754 (Ind. App. 1979). The ruling that found that a dentist's office is a legal home occupation is *Schwartz v. Chave*, 53 Misc. 2d 1007, 281 N.Y.S.2d 133 (1967).

7. *Nutini v. Zoning Bd. of Review*, 82 A2d 88, (RI 1951); *Yocum v. Fell*, 129 Fla. 764, 176 So. 753 (1938); *Bond v. Cook*, 237 AD 229, 262 N.Y.S. 199 (1932).

8. *Lerner v. Bloomfield Township*, 106 Mich. App. 809,308 N.W.2d 701 (1981); *City of Beverly Hills v. Brady*, 34 Cal. 2d 854, 215 P2d 460 (1950) *affd*. 205 P2d 1088 (1949); *Matter of Eisner,* 12 A.D.2d 786, 209 N.Y.S.2d 673 (1961); *City of Aberdeen v. Hermmann*, 301 N.W.2d 674 (S.D. 1981); *Deshazo v. City of Huntsville*, 416 So.2d 1100 (Ala. Crim. App. 1982); and *People v. Daly*, 28 N.Y.S.2d 603 (1941).

9. *County of DuPage v. Elliott*, 85 Ill. App. 3d 225, 40 Ill. Dec.586, 406 N.E,2d 592 (1980); *City of Rockford v. Eisenstein*, 63 Ill. App. 2d 128, 211 N.E.2d 130 (1965); *Village of Riverside v. Kuhne*, 335 Ill. App. 547, 82 N.E.2d 500 (1948); *Baker v. Town of Woolwich,* 517 A2d 64 Me. (1986).

10. *Muskegon Heights v. Wilson*, 363 Mich. 263, 109 NW2d 768 (1961).

LIST OF REFERENCES

Allen, Frederick. 1984. "Performance Standards for Home Occupations." *PAS Memo*, January.

American Society of Planning Officials. 1953. *Zoning Regulation of Home Occupations.* Planning Advisory Service Report No. 54. Chicago: American Planning Association, September.

American Planning Association, 1984. "Zoning for Home Occupations." *Zoning News*, March.

Anderson, Robert M. 1968. *American Law of Zoning*. San Francisco, Calif.: The Bancroft-Whitney Company.

Arccordino, John. 1997. "Home-Based Business and Welfare Reform: The Case of the GVM Market in Richmond, Virginia." *News & Views*. Chicago: Economic Development Division, American Planning Association.

Bassett, E.M. 1940. *Zoning: The Law Administration and Court Decisions During the First Twenty Years*. New York: The Russell Sage Foundation.

Bennett, Julie. 1999. "Home Bodies." *Planning*, May.

Butler, JoAnn, and Judith Getzels. 1985. *Home Occupation Ordinances*. Planning Advisory Service Report No. 391. Chicago: American Planning Association, October.

Dennison, Mark S. 1996. "Home Occupations as Accessory Uses." *Zoning News*, January.

Economic Development Division, American Planning Association. 1997. "Home-Based Work and Zoning." *News & Views*. Chicago.

Frank, Michael. 1993. "Homework: A Proposal to Solve the Dilemmas Caused by Changing Work Patterns." *Planning*, June.

Handy, Susan and Patricia Mokhtatian. 1995. "Planning For Telecommuting–Measurement and Policy Issues." *Journal of the American Planning Association.*

Hotch, Ripley. 1995. "Beyond Nuts an Bolts." *Nation's Business*, February.

Kennedy, Carolyn. 1991. "When Home Is Where the Business Is." *Zoning News*, December.

Rathkopf, Arden H., and Daren A. Rathkopf. 1992. *The Law of Zoning and Planning*. New York: Clark Boardman Callaghan.

Stafford, Kathryn, Alma Owen, and Suzanne Locker. 1997. "Home-Based Work and the Community." *News & Views*. Chicago, Economic Development Division of the American Planning Association.

Toner, William. 1976. *Planning for Home Occupations*. Planning Advisory Service Report No. 316. Chicago: American Planning Association, September.

Vizard, Mary McAleer. 1993. "Home Business Outlaws." *Home Office Computing*, February.